Sojourner TRUTH

by **GWENYTH SWAIN**
illustrated by **MATTHEW ARCHAMBAULT**

On My Own
BIOGRAPHY

Carolrhoda Books, Inc./Minneapolis

Photograph on p. 46, Library of Congress, LC-Z62-119343.
Quotations: pp. 10, 38, Sojourner Truth. *Narrative of Sojourner Truth*. ed. Margaret
Washington. New York: New York University Press, 1993; pp. 24, 32, 33, 47, Carleton
Mabee. *Sojourner Truth: Slave, Prophet, Legend*. New York: New York University Press,
1993; pp. 26, 27, Harriet Beecher Stowe. "Sojourner Truth, the Libyan Sibyl." *Atlantic II*,
April 1863.

This book is available in two editions:
Library binding by Carolrhoda Books, Inc., a division of Lerner Publishing Group
Soft cover by First Avenue Editions, an imprint of Lerner Publishing Group
241 First Avenue North
Minneapolis, MN 55401 U.S.A.

Website address: www.lernerbooks.com

Library of Congress Cataloging-in-Publication Data

Swain, Gwenyth, 1961–
    Sojourner Truth / by Gwenyth Swain.
        p.   cm. — (On my own biography)
    Summary: Describes the life of Sojourner Truth, an abolitionist who was herself a
former slave.
    ISBN: 1–57505–651–8 (lib. bdg. : alk. paper)
    ISBN: 1–57505–827–8 (pbk : alk. paper)
    1. Truth, Sojourner, d. 1883—Juvenile literature. 2. African American abolitionists—
Biography—Juvenile literature. 3. African American women—Biography—Juvenile
literature. 4. Abolitionists—United States—Biography—Juvenile literature. 5. Social
reformers—United States—Biography—Juvenile literature. [1. Truth, Sojourner,
d. 1883. 2. Abolitionists. 3. Reformers. 4. African Americans—Biography.
5. Women—Biography.] I. Title. II. Series.
    E185.97.T8S93 2005
    306.3'62'092—dc22   2003012512

Manufactured in the United States of America
1 2 3 4 5 6 – DP – 10 09 08 07 06 05

To my mother
—G.S.

To my wife, Melissa, and daughter Isabella
—M.A.

Isabella

Isabella was born about 1797.

People called her Bell for short.

But there was nothing short about her.

She grew tall and straight like her father.

He was called Bomefree,

the Dutch word for tree.

Bell's mother was called Mau-mau (Dutch
for mama) and Bett (short for Elizabeth).
Bell had many brothers and sisters.
But only brother Peter lived with her and
Bomefree and Mau-mau.

Bell's family didn't own the house
they lived in.
They didn't even own the hard cellar floor
they ate and slept on.
Instead, Charles Hardenbergh owned Bell
and her family.
He owned them just as he owned the big
stone house in Hurley, New York.

He owned them just as he owned
a flock of sheep.
He owned them just as he owned his
long-tailed coat and wide-brimmed hat.
Bell and her family were his slaves.
They were Dutch-speaking slaves.
They lived in what was the Dutch part of
New York State.

Winters were long there.

Ice coated the nearby Hudson River.

Summers were short there.

But on warm nights, the stars shone bright.

Bell and Peter saw them shine

when they sat outside on their parents' laps.

Mau-mau and Bomefree were tired after

working for Master Hardenbergh.

Bell and Peter were tired too.

Even young slaves worked.

But they weren't too tired for stories.

Bomefree told stories of all his lost babies.

Those older children belonged to

other masters, far from Hurley.

They had been sold years before.

Bell knew them only from stories

told at night.

Bell's mother told stories too.

"My children," she'd say, "there is a God who hears and sees you."

Bell loved to hear Mau-mau tell of God, who lived in the sky.

"He will always hear and help you," Mau-mau said.

Bell thought about Mau-mau's friend God after Master died.

Farmer John Neely bought Bell and some
sheep from the Hardenberghs.
Someone else bought Peter.
Mau-mau and Bomefree were too old
to be worth money.
They were left to live on their own.
They had no place to work or live.
Bell hardly ever saw them,
because she was so busy.

She was only nine but worked hard
all day long.

She tried her best to please her new master
and mistress.

But they spoke only English.

Bell knew only Dutch.

She never understood half the things
she did wrong.

She never forgot the beatings they gave her
to make her do right.

Bell talked to God when she thought
Master Neely couldn't hear.
She wasn't sure if God heard her.
But one day, a man asked to buy her.
This new master made her work harder
than before.
But he didn't beat her.
He treated her well enough that Bell
decided God had listened.

Finding Freedom

When Bell was 13, she was sold
to another master.
Master John Dumont was proud
of his young slave.
She did the work of a grown man.
Soon she grew as big as a man, standing
nearly six feet tall.

Bell was still a teenager when her first child, Diana, was born.

Master Dumont was pleased.

The baby was his property, to keep or sell.

Babies Peter and Elizabeth soon followed, making Master even happier.

Then Bell heard the news about freedom.

It was coming for slaves in New York State.

They would be free
on Independence Day 1827.
The law said so.
Once Bell knew freedom was coming,
she couldn't wait.
In 1825, she asked Master if she could have
her freedom a year early.
Master agreed, as long as Bell worked hard.
That year, Bell did her usual work
unusually well.

She bound the wheat
and loaded Master's wagon.
She washed Mistress's clothes
and cooked the meals.
She sheared the sheep and spun the wool
into thread.
The time came for Bell to be free.
But Master changed his mind.

Bell had shown how much she could do.

How could he let her go?

Bell loved truth almost more than freedom.

It hurt that Master had lied to her.

It hurt to see her own Independence Day
pass and still be a slave.

Bell did what Mau-mau told her to do
years before.

She talked to God, who lived in the sky.

With God's help, Bell made up her mind.

She wouldn't wait for Master to free her.

She wouldn't wait for the state of New York
to free her.

Bell rose early one crisp morning, when the
leaves were turning color.

She didn't wake her older children.

She hoped to come back for them soon.

She carried her new baby in one arm.

In the other, she carried a sack
of clothes and food.

Before Master awoke, Bell slipped away.

She found freedom.

Finding a New Name

Bell didn't know it, but she was
on a long journey.
For a time, she lived in New York City
and worked as a maid.
But Bell didn't want to be a maid forever.
She dreamed of showing others how
to talk to God.
She dreamed of being a preacher.

It was hard to preach
if you couldn't read the Bible.
Bell had never learned to read,
no matter how she'd tried.
"The letters all got mixed up," she said,
"and I couldn't straighten them out."

She asked grown-ups to read her the Bible.

They read the words

and told Bell what they meant.

Bell wanted to make up her own mind.

She asked children to read the Bible to her.

Children never told her what to think.

By 1843, Bell was more than 40 years old.

She was ready to preach.

She took a ferry to Brooklyn, New York.

Along the way, she found a new name

to fit her new life.

A sojourner is a person who goes from

place to place.

God, Bell believed, told her

to call herself Sojourner.

"Because," she said, "I was to travel up an'

down the land."

But free people had two names.
While she was preaching in Long Island,
she chose the last name Truth.
"Because," she said, "I was to declare truth
to the people."

Most folks thought women
belonged at home.
Most folks didn't think a slave was worth
listening to.
But Sojourner Truth had a strong voice
and an even stronger faith.
She gathered crowds around her.

While she preached, the world changed.

By 1850, slavery had ended in the North.

But it was still strong in the South.

In the South, slave families were still being torn apart.

Slaves were still being beaten.

Slaves were still dreaming of freedom.

Some people in the North tried to help.

They spoke out about the horrors of slavery.

They demanded that slavery end.

Most speakers were white people.

But not Sojourner Truth.

She talked about how *it felt* to be a slave.

Sojourner brought the truth about slavery
to crowds across the land.

She talked about the sting of Master's whip
on her back.

But she didn't cry at the memory.

She stood tall and proud.

She wore a plain dark dress and
wrapped her head in a clean white turban.

When she spoke, Sojourner Truth made
people think and sometimes laugh.
She also sang songs about God.
"In every day of trouble," she sang,
"I'll raise my thoughts on high."
Maybe others could say it better.

But no one said it quite like
Sojourner Truth.
"Life is a hard battle anyway," she told
a friend, "and if we can laugh and sing a
little as we fight the good fight of freedom,
it makes it all go easier."

Traveling On

Sojourner Truth traveled thousands of
miles, speaking against slavery.
But slavery wasn't the only wrong she saw.
Free women—black and white—
weren't treated as well as men.

Free women could not vote.
In many states, they could not
own property.
They were paid less than men were
for the same work.
Soon Sojourner was speaking out
for women's rights.

Many men said women were weak
and shouldn't be paid as much as men.
But Sojourner Truth raised her arms
and showed off her strong muscles.
"I have plowed and reaped and husked
and chopped and mowed," she said, "and
can any man do more than that?"

No matter where she was,
Sojourner fought for
people's rights.
In Washington, D.C., horsecars
would not stop for black passengers.
That didn't stop Sojourner Truth.
She ran after the cars. She yelled
until they had to stop.
She and others forced the horsecars to stop
for all passengers.

When she rode down the streets of
Washington, Sojourner didn't look
at buildings and monuments.
She looked at the people in the horsecars.
"The insides of the cars," she said happily,
"looked like pepper and salt."

Not every battle was so easy.

Slavery did not end until a long and terrible
war nearly tore the country apart.

Women could not vote until 1920,
long after Sojourner Truth had died.
Women are still sometimes paid less than
men for the same work.
But setbacks and sorrows never stopped
Sojourner Truth.

In 1857, she bought a little house of her own
to share with her grown daughters.
But Sojourner still kept on traveling
and fighting.
The going was not easy.
The road she traveled was long and hard.
But until she died, Sojourner Truth
brought truth to the people.

Afterword

Sojourner Truth was an extraordinary woman. In her time, few women spoke in public. And almost no former slaves gave speeches. Few whites—in the North or the South—thought black slaves had much to say. After all, slaves like Sojourner Truth were uneducated. But Sojourner Truth never let her sex, her lack of education, or the color of her skin stop her. And by being unstoppable, she was an inspiration to people in her time and ever since.

Sojourner Truth lived before radio or television, so we can only imagine what she sounded and looked like as a speaker. But those who heard her were overwhelmed by the simple power of her words, her tall form, and her good humor. "I don't read such small stuff as letters," she once said, "I read men and nations." Sojourner Truth may well have had a reading disability. But she was a great reader of people. Whenever she spoke, she shared what she had learned about people as a slave and as a woman. And she urged her fellow Americans to "fight the good fight" of freedom, justice, and fairness one step at a time.

Important Dates

1797—Isabella is born at about this time to James (Bomefree) and Elizabeth (Mau-mau Bett), in Hurley, New York. Because she is a slave, no official record is made of her birth.

1806—At about this time, Bell becomes the slave of John Neely in Kingston, New York.

1810–26—Bell is the slave of John Dumont, of New Paltz, New York. She marries and gives birth to five children, one of whom dies as a baby. In the fall of 1826, she takes her youngest child and walks to freedom.

1827—On July 4, all New York slaves are officially freed.

1829–43—The former slave Bell works as a maid in New York City and trains to be a preacher. In June of 1843, using the name Sojourner Truth, she begins preaching.

1850—Sojourner begins to speak out against slavery and for women's rights. She also publishes the story of her life, called the *Narrative of Sojourner Truth.*

1857—Sojourner buys a home near Battle Creek, Michigan.

1865—Sojourner forces horsecars in Washington, D.C., to stop for black passengers.

1879—Sojourner travels to Kansas to help former southern slaves build new lives there.

1883—Sojourner Truth dies on November 26 at her home in Battle Creek, Michigan.